Tee Off!

You Can Play Golf

by Nick Fauchald
illustrated by Ronnie Rooney

Special thanks to our advisers for their expertise:

Kevin McManemin
United States Golf Association, Far Hills, New Jersey

Susan Kesselring, M.A., Literacy Educator
Rosemount–Apple Valley–Eagan (Minnesota) School District

PICTURE WINDOW BOOKS
Minneapolis, Minnesota

Editorial Director: Carol Jones

Managing Editor: Catherine Neitge

Creative Director: Keith Griffin

Editor: Jill Kalz

Story Consultant: Terry Flaherty

Designer: Joe Anderson

Page Production: Picture Window Books

The illustrations in this book were created with acrylics.

Picture Window Books

5115 Excelsior Boulevard

Suite 232

Minneapolis, MN 55416

877-845-8392

www.picturewindowbooks.com

Printed in the United States of America.

Library of Congress Cataloging-in-Publication Data

Fauchald, Nick.

Tee off! You can play golf / by Nick Fauchald ; illustrated by Ronnie Rooney.

p. cm. — (Game day)

Includes bibliographical references and index.

ISBN 1-4048-1155-9 (hardcover)

1. Golf—Juvenile literature. I. Title: Tee off!. II. Title: You can play golf.

III. Rooney, Ronnie. IV. Title.

GV968.F38 2006

796.352—dc22   2005004271

Golf is a challenging sport that can be played by people of all ages and skill levels. The object of the game is to hit a ball into a hole in as few shots as possible. It sounds easy, but it's not! A golf course is very large and may be full of trees, sand bunkers, and bodies of water that you must avoid.

It's a bright, sunny day. You and your friend Joanna are going to your first golf lesson. Mom drives both of you to the golf course. Your instructor, Eddie, is already waiting for you. Let's get started!

A golf course is divided into areas called holes. Most courses have 18, but some have only nine. The first shot on each hole is hit from the tee box. Your target, the hole (or cup), is located on a circle of very short grass called the green. The area between the tee box and the green is called the fairway.

"Golf clubs, golf balls, and tees are all you need to play golf," Eddie says. "Clubs are sticks used to hit the ball. Tees are little pegs that hold the ball up off the ground to make it easier to hit."

Eddie first shows you how to grip the golf clubs. He places your feet shoulder-width apart. He makes sure your knees are slightly bent. Joanna lines her feet up the same way.

Position your hands on the golf club like you would put them on a baseball bat—with your hands together and knuckles lined up. If you're right-handed, your right hand should be closer to the head (the bulb-shaped end) of the club. Some players lock or overlap their fingers.

7

You and Joanna bring your arms back as far as you can, your hands behind your heads. You swing through and let your arms follow. "Nice practice swings!" Eddie says. "Make sure you keep your head down, though, so you can keep your eyes on the ball."

When you swing a golf club, your feet shouldn't move around too much. You should never feel like you're going to fall over. At first, don't worry about where the ball goes. When you get used to swinging the club, pick a target in the distance and try to hit the ball toward it.

Eddie sets a ball down in front of you. He centers it between your feet. You practice hitting with your irons. Joanna practices, too.

Eddie shows you and Joanna how to tee up the ball and hit it with the driver. "You need to stand back a little farther from the ball because the driver is the longest golf club of all," Eddie says. You take a swing— WHACK!—and watch the ball soar into the air. "Hitting the ball off the tee is called 'teeing off.'"

Irons are golf clubs with metal heads. Irons can be used anywhere except on the green. Each iron is given a different number. As you get closer to the hole, you use irons with higher numbers. These are shorter and will hit the ball higher into the air. The driver, or wood, is a club with a wooden head. It's used to tee off.

Putting is a very important part of golf, but it can be difficult to learn. Luckily, it's easy to practice—you can practice at a mini-golf park or even on the carpet at home (if your parents say it's OK)!

Next, Eddie takes you and Joanna to the practice green. Other golfers are practicing their putting. "The putter is a special golf club used for putting," Eddie says. "Hold it like you do the other clubs, but stand closer to the ball so your head and eyes are directly above the ball."

You picture an imaginary line running from the golf ball to the cup. You gently rock your arms back then forward and try to hit the ball down that line.

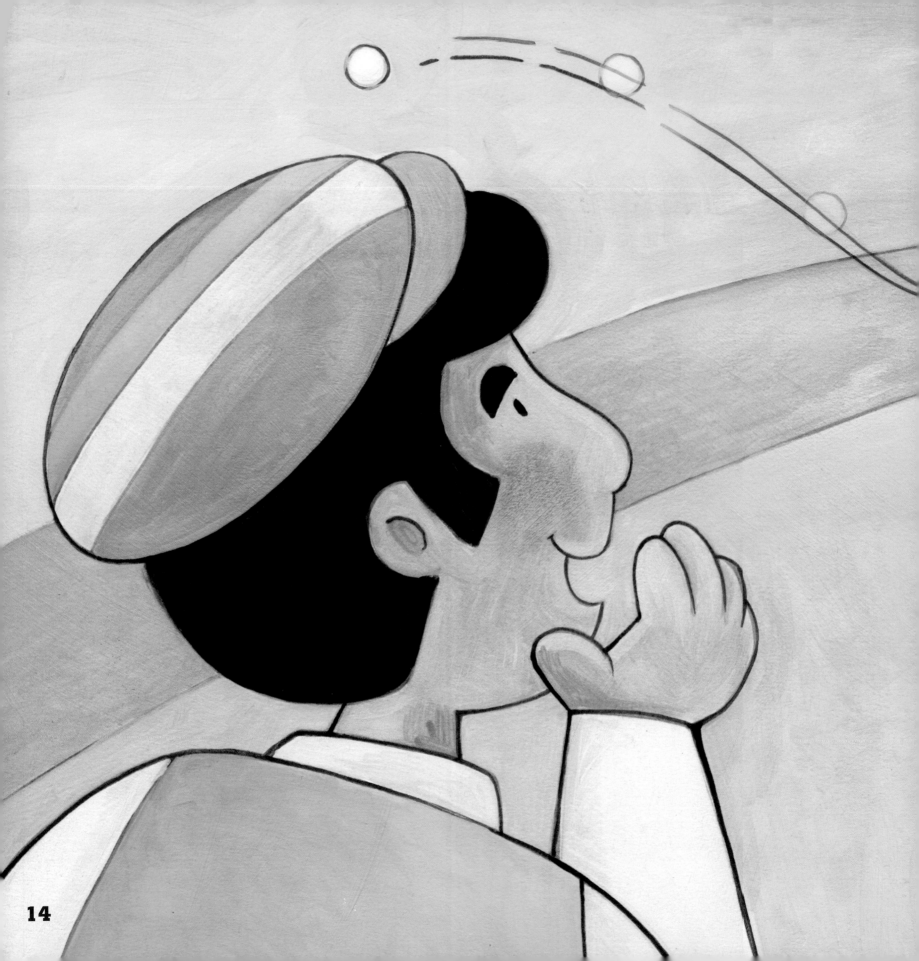

After a few more putts, the three of you walk to the main area of the golf course. Joanna tees up her ball in the tee-off area called the tee box. She swings her driver—WHOOSH!—and misses the ball.

"That's OK. Try again," Eddie says. Joanna connects on her second swing, and the ball sails onto the fairway.

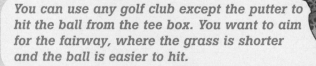

You can use any golf club except the putter to hit the ball from the tee box. You want to aim for the fairway, where the grass is shorter and the ball is easier to hit.

Now it's your turn. WHACK! Your ball bounces down the side of the fairway and into a sand bunker.

"Hitting out of a sand bunker is almost like hitting a regular shot," Eddie says. "But instead of hitting the ball, you want to hit the sand directly behind the ball." You take a swing and watch as the ball flies out, along with a cloud of sand.

It's very important to have good manners on the golf course. Be quiet and stand still when other players are hitting. If your ball goes into a sand bunker, rake away your footprints before you leave. If your ball makes a divot, ask an adult to show you how to repair it.

You and Joanna take turns hitting your balls. The two of you aim for the flag sticking out of the cup. After a few shots, you are both on the green.

Joanna's ball is farther away from the cup, so she goes first. She carefully lines up her putt and swings ... IT'S IN THE HOLE!

Each hole on a golf course is given a number rating called par. This number is the number of strokes, or swings, an expert golfer would probably take to get the ball into the cup. Most holes are 3, 4, or 5 par.

Now it's your turn. You carefully line up your putt. You rock the golf club back and then forward. The ball travels down its imaginary path ... all the way into the bottom of the cup.

Nice putt! You're learning how to play golf!

Diagram of a Golf Course

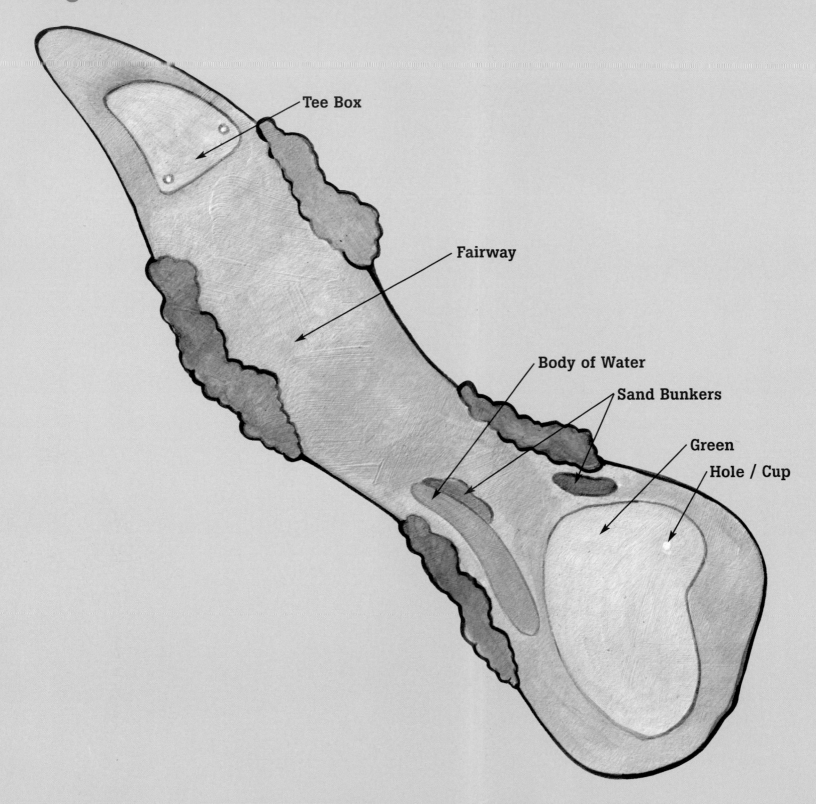

Tee Box

Fairway

Body of Water

Sand Bunkers

Green

Hole / Cup

FUN FACTS

 Some historians trace the origins of golf back to the Netherlands (the Dutch word *kolf* means "club"). Others trace the origins back 2,000 years to Ancient Rome, where boys played a golf-like game in the streets with a bent stick and a ball made from feathers. The modern game of golf, however, was developed in Scotland as early as the 12th century.

The British golfer Joyce Wethered, winner of four British Women's Amateur Championships and five English Ladies' Championships, is often considered the greatest female golfer in the history of the game.

Jack Nicklaus, who has won 20 major championships, is one of the greatest golfers of all time.

Professional golfer Tiger Woods started playing golf in his garage when he was just 11 months old. In 1997, Woods became the youngest player ever to win the Masters Tournament. He was 21 years old.

GLOSSARY

divot—a piece of grass loosened by the swing of a golf club

driver—the largest, most powerful golf club; a driver is also called a wood

fairway—the area of a golf course between the tee box and the green

green—the area of a golf course where the hole is located; the grass on a green is cut very short so the ball rolls more easily

irons—the clubs used most often in golf; irons are usually made of steel

putting—hitting a golf ball short distances on the green so it rolls into or near the cup; a putter is a special golf club used just for putting

sand bunker—a sand trap

tee—a peg used on the tee box to hold the ball above the ground so it is easier to hit

TO LEARN MORE

At the Library

Ditchfield, Christin. *Golf.* Danbury, Conn.: Children's Press, 2003.

Simmons, Richard. *Golf.* New York: Dorling Kindersley Publishing, 2001.

Will, Sandra. *Golf for Fun!* Minneapolis: Compass Point Books, 2003.

On the Web

FactHound offers a safe, fun way to find Web sites related to this book.
All of the sites on FactHound have been researched by our staff.

http://www.facthound.com

1. Visit the FactHound home page.
2. Enter a search word related to this book,
   or type in this special code: 1404811559.
3. Click on the FETCH IT button.

Your trusty FactHound will fetch the best sites for you!

INDEX

Look for all the books in the Game Day series:

Batter Up! You Can Play Softball

Bump! Set! Spike! You Can Play Volleyball

Face Off! You Can Play Hockey

Jump Ball! You Can Play Basketball

Nice Hit! You Can Play Baseball

Score! You Can Play Soccer

Tee Off! You Can Play Golf

Touchdown! You Can Play Football